Angels

QUOTATIONS FROM THE
WRITINGS OF ELLEN G. WHITE

Compiled by Ken & Debby Wade

Pacific Press® Publishing Association
Nampa, Idaho
Oshawa, Ontario, Canada

Compiled by Ken and Debby Wade
Designed by Linda Criswell
Cover photo by Mark Lisk
Typeset in 14/16.8 Adobe Garamond

Copyright 1995
Pacific Press® Publishing Association
Printed in United States of America
All Rights Reserved

White, Ellen Gould Harmon, 1827-1915
    Angels : quotations from the writings of Ellen G. White / compilers, Ken and Debby Wade
      p.   cm.
    ISBN 0-8163-1310-5 (alk. paper)
    1. Angels—Quotations, maxims, etc. 2. Seventh-day Adventists—Doctrines—Quotations, maxims, etc. I. Wade, Kenneth R., 1951-. II. Wade, Debby, 1951- . III. Title.
    BT966.2.W55 1995
    235'.3—dc20

95-39713
CIP

97 98 99 • 5 4 3 2

INTRODUCTION

What would it be like to receive messages directly from heaven? To be able to see the angels who wing their way back and forth, entering the very throne room of God, and then coming to earth to guide, protect, and encourage God's people?

Back in 1844, a young woman by the name of Ellen Harmon began receiving visions of heaven and of events on this earth. Often the curtain that hides the spiritual world from our view was drawn back, and she could actually see the ministry of angels sent to our aid. Over the years, this woman, whose married name was Ellen White, wrote many thousands of pages of material based on her visions and insights.

Here, drawn from the vast resource of her preserved writings, are some of the most encouraging passages regarding the ministry of angels.

This is not an exhaustive list. It is not intended as a research tool, but simply as an encouragement to those who may feel that they face life alone, those who would like to know more about the ministry of angels, those who would like to cooperate with angels in missions of mercy, and those who would like to encourage others.

The selections are organized randomly rather than topically, with the intention that a person picking up the book may experience the serendipity of discovering a new thought to bless a day's meditation.

*W*hen the earthborn children know it not,
they have angels of light as their companions.

6T 366

Angels are God's ministers,
radiant with the light ever flowing from His presence
and speeding on rapid wing to execute His will.

PP 34

*H*uman agencies are the hands
of heavenly instrumentalities,
for heavenly angels employ human hands
in practical ministry.

ML 305

$\mathcal{T}$oday . . . heavenly messengers are passing through
the length and breadth of the land,
seeking to comfort the sorrowing,
to protect the impenitent,
to win the hearts of men to Christ.
We cannot see them personally;
nevertheless they are with us,
guiding, directing, protecting.

ML 303

*W*hen unconsciously we are in danger
of exerting a wrong influence,
the angels will be by our side,
prompting us to a better course,
choosing words for us, and influencing our actions.

ML 302

The very angels who, when Satan was seeking
the supremacy, fought the battle in the heavenly courts
and triumphed on the side of God,
the very angels who shouted for joy over the creation
of our world and its sinless inhabitants,
the angels who witnessed the fall of man and his expulsion
from his Eden home—these very heavenly messengers
are most intensely interested to work in union
with the fallen, redeemed race for the salvation of human
beings perishing in their sins.

6T 456

$\mathcal{W}$e cannot behold their forms with our natural sight;
only by spiritual vision can we discern heavenly things.

ML 303

$\mathcal{I}$ have seen the tender love that God has
for His people,
and it is very great.
I saw angels over the saints
with their wings spread about them.

EW 39

Scarcely any of us realize that angels are about us;
and these precious angels,
who minister to those who shall be heirs of salvation,
are saving from us
many, many temptations and difficulties.

RH 5 August 1890

All who engage in ministry are God's helping hand.
They are co-workers with the angels; rather,
they are the human agencies
through whom the angels accomplish their mission.
Angels speak through their voices,
and work by their hands.

Ed 271

The angels of God are ever near your little ones.

AH 432

$\mathscr{T}$hose fallen and degraded by sin and crime may,
through the merits of the Saviour,
be exalted to a position
but little lower than that of the angels.

4T 294

As the echo of the angels' song
is awakened in our earthly homes,
hearts will be drawn closer to the heavenly singers.
Heaven's communion begins on earth.
We learn here the keynote of its praise.

Ed 168

The home that is beautified by love, sympathy,
and tenderness is a place that angels love to visit,
and where God is glorified.

AH 19

Strength, grace, and glory
have been provided through Christ,
to be brought by ministering angels
to the heirs of salvation.

2T 453

The Master's message
must be declared in the Master's spirit.
Our only safety is in keeping our thoughts and impulses
under the control of the Great Teacher.
Angels of God will give to every true worker
a rich experience in doing this.

7T 266

As night drew on,
soldiers were stationed to guard the Saviour's resting place,
while angels, unseen, hovered above the sacred spot.
The night wore slowly away, and while it was yet dark,
the watching angels knew that the time
for the release of God's dear Son,
their loved Commander, had nearly come.

EW 181

The Roman guard saw the angels,
and fell as dead men to the ground.
One angel rolled back the stone in triumph,
and with a clear and mighty voice, cried out,
Thou Son of God! Thy Father calls thee! Come forth!!
Death could hold dominion over him no longer.
Jesus arose from the dead.

1SG 66

A young man clothed in shining garments
was sitting by the tomb.
It was the angel who had rolled away the stone.
He had taken the guise of humanity
that he might not alarm these friends of Jesus.

DA 788, 789

These angels were of the company that had been waiting
in a shining cloud to escort Jesus to His heavenly home.
The most exalted of the angel throng,
they were the two who had come to the tomb
at Christ's resurrection,
and they had been with Him
throughout His life on earth.

DA 832

As you try to make plain the truths of salvation,
and point the children to Christ as a personal Saviour,
angels will be by your side.

DA 517

Those who labor for the good of others
are working in union with the heavenly angels.
They have their constant companionship,
their unceasing ministry.

6T 307, 308

Angelic agencies, though invisible,
are cooperating with visible human agencies,
forming a relief association with men.
Is there not something stimulating and inspiring
in this thought that the human agent stands
as the visible instrument
to confer the blessings of angelic agencies?

ML 305

*Sometimes the heavenly intelligences
draw aside the curtain that hides the unseen world,
that our minds may be withdrawn from the hurry and rush,
and consider that there are witnesses to all we do and say,
when engaged in business,
or when we think ourselves alone.*

SD 37

Angels of God wafted their wings
over the persecuted ones,
while Satan and his angels
were seeking to press their darkness around them,
to lead them to reject the light from heaven.

EW 241

*L*ong delays tire the angels.
It is even more excusable to make a wrong decision
sometimes than to be continually in a wavering position,
to be hesitating, sometimes inclined in one direction,
then in another.

3T 497

Teachers should work circumspectly.
Those who are often with God in prayer,
have holy angels by their side.
The atmosphere that surrounds their souls is pure and holy;
for their whole soul is imbued
with the sanctifying influence of the Spirit of God.

FE 430

These angels of light
create a heavenly atmosphere about the soul,
lifting us toward the unseen and the eternal.
We cannot behold their forms with our natural sight;
only by spiritual vision can we discern heavenly things.
The spiritual ear alone
can hear the harmony of heavenly voices.

AA 153

*O*ur determined efforts to bring souls
to a knowledge of the truth for this time
will be seconded by holy angels,
and many souls will be saved.

Ev 38

2—ANGELS

If those who have erred continue to plead,
and in deep humility confess their wrongs,
angels who excel in strength will prevail
and wrench them from the power of the evil angels.

RH 18 February 1862

Angels,
who will do for you what you can not do for yourselves,
are waiting for your co-operation.
They are waiting for you
to respond to the drawing of Christ.

SD 36

The position of the cherubim,
with their faces turned toward each other,
and looking reverently downward toward the ark,
represented the reverence with which the heavenly host
regard the law of God
and their interest in the plan of redemption.

PP 348, 349

Though enemies may thrust them into prison,
yet dungeon walls cannot cut off the communication
between their souls and Christ.
One who sees their every weakness,
who is acquainted with every trial,
is above all earthly powers;
and angels will come to them in lonely cells,
bringing light and peace from heaven.

GC 627

_L_et your conversation, your music,
your songs all praise Him who has done so much for us.
Praise God here, and then you will be fitted
to join the heavenly choir
when you enter the city of God.

_ML 91_

All the resources of heaven
are at the command of those who are seeking
to save the lost.
Angels will help you to reach
the most careless and the most hardened.
And when one is brought back to God,
all heaven is made glad.

COL 197

Seraphs and cherubs touch their golden harps,
and sing praises to God and the Lamb
for their mercy and loving-kindness
to the children of men.

COL 197

$\mathcal{I}$t is the work of the angels to come close to the tried,
the suffering, the tempted.
They labor untiringly in behalf of those
for whom Christ died.

AA 153, 154

I saw that God has His agents,
even among the rulers. . . .
When Satan works through his agents,
propositions are made, that, if carried out,
would impede the work of God and produce great evil.
The good angels move upon these agents of God
to oppose such propositions with strong reasons. . . .
A few of God's agents will have power
to bear down a great mass of evil.

1T 203

$\mathcal{B}$y sincere, earnest prayer
parents should make a hedge about their children.
They should pray with full faith
that God will abide with them,
and that holy angels will guard them and their children
from Satan's cruel power.

ML 31

These heavenly watchers shield the righteous
from the power of the wicked one.

ML 302

The Lord never forsakes His faithful messengers.
He sends to their aid heavenly agencies
and accompanies their labors with the power of His Holy
Spirit to convince and to convert.

Ev 38

All the heavenly angels are at the service of the humble,
believing people of God;
and as the Lord's army of workers here below
sing their songs of praise,
the choir above join with them
in ascribing praise to God and to His Son.

AA 154

All who desire the cooperation
of the heavenly messengers
must work in unison with them.
Those who have the unction from on high
will in all their efforts encourage order, discipline,
and union of action,
and then the angels of God can cooperate with them.

TM 28

If we see no necessity for harmonious action,
and are disorderly, undisciplined,
and disorganized in our course of action,
angels, who are thoroughly organized
and move in perfect order,
cannot work for us successfully.
They turn away in grief,
for they are not authorized to bless confusion, distraction,
and disorganization.

TM 28

Some are assailed in their flight
from the cities and villages;
but the swords raised against them break
and fall powerless as a straw.
Others are defended by angels in the form of men of war.

GC 631

$\mathcal{A}$ guardian angel is appointed
to every follower of Christ.

ML 302

Believers on the earth and the beings in heaven
who have never fallen constitute one church.
Every heavenly intelligence is interested
in the assemblies of the saints
who on earth meet to worship God.

6T 366

So angels are ever engaged
in working for the happiness of others.
This is their joy.
That which selfish hearts would regard
as humiliating service,
ministering to those who are wretched
and in every way inferior in character and rank,
is the work of sinless angels.

SC 77

I was shown those whom I had before seen
weeping and praying in agony of spirit.
The company of guardian angels around them
had been doubled, and they were clothed
with an armor from their head to their feet.

Ed 270

$\mathcal{T}$he angels love to bow before God;
they love to be near Him.
They regard communion with God as their highest joy;
and yet the children of earth,
who need so much the help that God only can give,
seem satisfied to walk without the light of His Spirit,
the companionship of His presence.

SC 94

$\mathcal{T}$he angels all wear the yoke of obedience.
They are the appointed messengers of Him
who is the Commander of all heaven.

5BC 1136

*H*eavenly angels watch the careworn mother,
noting the burdens she carries day by day.
Her name may not have been heard in the world,
but it is written in the Lamb's book of life.

CT 144

Those who in heaven join with the angelic choir
in their anthem of praise
must learn on earth the song of heaven,
the keynote of which is thanksgiving.

7T 244

*O*nly as they were united with Christ
could the disciples hope to have the accompanying power
of the Holy Spirit and the co-operation of angels
of heaven. . . . As they should continue to labor unitedly,
heavenly messengers would go before them,
opening the way;
hearts would be prepared for the reception of truth,
and many would be won to Christ.

AA 90, 91

*A*ngels are constantly ascending and descending
this ladder of shining brightness,
bearing the prayers of the needy and distressed
to the Father above,
and bringing blessing and hope, courage and help,
to the children of men.

AA 153

"The entrance of Thy words giveth light;
it giveth understanding unto the simple."
Angels stand beside the searcher of the Scriptures,
to impress and illuminate the mind.

MYP 257

Angels actually come to our world.
Nor are they always invisible.
They sometimes veil their angelic appearance,
and appearing as men,
they converse with and enlighten human beings.

ML 304

$\mathcal{T}$hus God's people,
exposed to the deceptive power
and unsleeping malice of the prince of darkness,
and in conflict with all the forces of evil,
are assured of the unceasing
guardianship of heavenly angels.

GC 513

In searching the Scriptures
there is need of great humility of mind
and contrition of heart,
of seeking earnestly unto God.
Those who come in a lowly spirit,
seeking for truth,
will be aided in their search by the angels of God.

CSW 37

About the throne gathered the holy angels,
a vast, unnumbered throng.

PP 36

*T*hese heavenly beings are ministering angels,
and they frequently disguise themselves
in the form of human beings,
and as strangers
converse with those
who are engaged in the work of God.

SD 37

3—ANGELS

*O*ur first parents . . . were to enjoy communion
with God and with holy angels.

PP 48

$\mathcal{T}$he happiness of the angelic host
consisted in their perfect obedience to law.
Each had his special work assigned him;
and until Satan rebelled, there had been perfect order
and harmonious action in Heaven.

1SP 23

$\mathcal{D}$o you humbly, heartily make known your wants
to your heavenly Father?
If so, angels mark your prayers,
and if these prayers have not gone forth out of feigned lips,
when you are in danger of unconsciously doing wrong and
exerting an influence which will lead others to do wrong,
your guardian angel will be by your side,
prompting you to a better course,
choosing your words for you,
and influencing your actions.

3T 363, 364

$\mathscr{I}$ saw the saints leaving the cities and villages,
and associating together in companies,
and living in the most solitary places.
Angels provided them food and water,
while the wicked were suffering from hunger and thirst.

EW 282

*H*uman workers, co-operating with heavenly agencies,
have the benefit of their education and experience.
As a means of education,
what "university course" can equal this?

Ed 271

$\mathscr{S}$ince there is decided sympathy
between heaven and earth,
and since God commissions angels to minister
unto all who are in need of help,
we know that if we do our part,
these heavenly representatives of omnipotent power
will give help in this time of need.

6T 461

As Elijah slept,
a soft touch and a pleasant voice awoke him.
He started up in terror, as if to flee,
fearing that the enemy had discovered him.
But the pitying face bending over him
was not the face of an enemy, but of a friend.
God had sent an angel from heaven
with food for His servant.

PK 166

$\mathcal{T}$he angels of God are clothed with a complete armor,
the panoply of heaven, and,
although surrounded with deadly foes,
fear nothing, for they are doing the will
of their loved Commander.

2SG 277

*A*ngels are ever present where they are most needed.
They are with those who have the hardest battles to fight,
with those who must battle against inclination
and hereditary tendencies,
whose home surroundings are the most discouraging.

ML 303

In their ministry the angels are not as servants,
but as sons.
There is perfect unity between them and their Creator.
Obedience is to them no drudgery.
Love for God makes their service a joy.

MB 109

Angels of heaven were beside the Samaritan
who cared for the wounded stranger.
Angels from the heavenly courts
stand by all who do God's service
in ministering to their fellow men.

COL 388

Each saint had an attending angel.
If the saints wept through discouragement,
or were in danger,
the angels that ever attended them
would fly quickly upward to carry the tidings,
and the angels in the city would cease to sing.
Then Jesus would commission another angel
to descend to encourage, watch over,
and try to keep them
from going out of the narrow path.

EW 39

The Egyptians dared to venture in the path
God had prepared for His people,
and angels of God went through their host
and removed their chariot wheels.

SR 124

A silent witness guards every soul that lives,
seeking to draw that soul to Christ.

6T 366

*U*nder God the angels are all-powerful.

DA 700

At the sound of fervent prayer,
Satan's whole host trembles. . . .
And when angels, all-powerful,
clothed with the armor of heaven,
come to the help of the fainting, pursued soul,
Satan and his host fall back,
well knowing that their battle is lost.

MYP 53

*H*eavenly angels are still working
in co-operation with human agencies.
The Holy Spirit is presenting every inducement
to constrain you to come. . . .
Angels are waiting to bear the tidings to heaven
that another lost sinner has been found.

COL 237

Angels are watching with intense interest
to see how man is dealing with his fellow men.
When they see one
manifest Christlike sympathy for the erring,
they press to his side
and bring to his remembrance words to speak
that will be as the bread of life to the soul.

COL 149

Then they shut the disciples up in a prison,
that the message of God
should no longer be given to the people,
but the angel of the Lord was there.
All heaven was looking upon them then,
and the angels are now looking upon those
who are living at this closing period of earth's history.

RH 22 April 1890

*A*ngels of God, that excel in strength,
are waiting for us to call them to our aid,
that our faith may not be eclipsed
by the fierceness of the conflict.

1SM 195,196

The spirit of ministry is the spirit of heaven,
and with every effort to develop and encourage it
angels will co-operate.

MH 401

Angels are sent on missions of mercy
to the children of God.
To Abraham, with promises of blessing;
to the gates of Sodom, to rescue righteous Lot
from its fiery doom;
to Elijah, as he was about to perish from weariness and
hunger in the desert; . . .
thus holy angels have, in all ages,
ministered to God's people.

GC 512

Angels attend Joseph and Mary
as they journey from their home in Nazareth
to the city of David.

DA 44

*B*efore the creation of man, angels were in existence;
for when the foundations of the earth were laid,
"the morning stars sang together,
and all the sons of God shouted for joy."

BEcho 23 September 1895

In working for perishing souls
you have the companionship of angels.
Thousands upon thousands,
and ten thousand times ten thousand angels
are waiting to co-operate with members of our churches
in communicating the light that God has generously given,
that a people may be prepared for the coming of Christ.

CM 110

$\mathcal{H}$e would sooner send every angel out of glory
to the relief of faithful souls,
to make a hedge about them,
than have them deceived and led away
by the lying wonders of Satan.

EW 88

*W*hile some are in the valley of decision,
angels are uniting with true, wholehearted servants
of Christ to help these needy souls.

ML 304

*K*neel before God, and plead with Him
for an understanding of His word.
Be sure that you know the real principles of the truth;
and then when you meet opponents,
it will not be in your own strength;
an angel of God will stand by your side,
to help in answering every question that may be asked.

GW 105

In all ages,
God has wrought through holy angels
for the succor and deliverance of His people.
Celestial beings have taken an active part
in the affairs of men.
They have appeared clothed in garments
that shone as the lightning;
they have come as men
in the garb of wayfarers.

GC 631

The angels of God are ever passing from earth to heaven,
and from heaven to earth.
The miracles of Christ for the afflicted and suffering
were wrought by the power of God
through the ministration of the angels.

DA 143

Ministering angels open the eyes of the mind and heart
to see wonderful things in the divine law,
in the natural world,
and in the eternal things revealed by the Holy Spirit.

ML 291

$\mathscr{A}$s we try to become acquainted with our heavenly
Father
through His word, angels will draw near,
our minds will be strengthened,
our characters will be elevated and refined.
We shall become more like our Saviour.

DA 70

4—ANGELS

There are angels who excel in strength
who will be with us in all our conflicts
if we will only be faithful.

3T 526

Could our spiritual vision be quickened,
we should see . . . angels flying swiftly
to aid these tempted ones,
who are standing as on the brink of a precipice.
The angels from heaven force back the hosts of evil
that encompass these souls,
and guide them to plant their feet
on the sure foundation.

MB 188, 189

Every redeemed one will understand
the ministry of angels in his own life.
The angel who was his guardian
from his earliest moment,
the angel who watched his steps
and covered his head in the day of peril,
the angel who was with him
in the valley of the shadow of death,

who marked his resting place,
who was the first to greet him
in the resurrection morning—
what will it be to hold converse with him,
and to learn the history of divine interposition
in the individual life,
of heavenly cooperation in every work for humanity!

Ed 305 (1903)

The ministering angels are passing through the churches, noting our faithfulness in our individual line of duty.

6BC 1060

$\mathcal{T}$hey studied the Bible, not from curiosity,
but in order that they might learn what had been written
concerning the promised Messiah.
Daily they searched the inspired records,
and as they compared scripture with scripture,
heavenly angels were beside them,
enlightening their minds and impressing their hearts.

AA 231

The angels appointed to minister to the children of God
have at all times access to His presence.

GC 513

There is perfect order and harmony in the Holy City.
All the angels that are commissioned
to visit the earth hold a golden card,
which they present to the angels at the gates of the city
as they pass in and out.

EW 39

$\mathcal{T}$he angels of heaven look upon the distress
of God's family upon the earth,
and they are prepared to co-operate with men
in relieving oppression and suffering.

DA 500

It is the greatest joy of the angels in heaven
to spread the shield of their tender love
over the souls who turn to God.
Their love for those for whom Christ died
is beyond measurement.

RH 26 January 1911

Angels are commissioned to watch in every family.
Each one has the watchcare of a holy angel.
These angels are invisible,
but sometimes they let their light shine
so distinctly that it is recognized.

3MR 305, 306

$\mathcal{B}$ut if the saints fixed their eyes
upon the prize before them
and glorified God by praising Him,
then the angels would bear the glad tidings to the city,
and the angels in the city would touch their golden harps
and sing with a loud voice, "Alleluia!"
and the heavenly arches would ring
with their lovely songs.

EW 39

Sometimes the heavenly intelligences
draw aside the curtain which hides the unseen world
that our thoughts may be withdrawn from the hurry
and rush of life to consider that there are unseen witnesses
to all we do or say.

COL 176

Angels pity these wandering ones.
Angels weep,
while human eyes are dry and hearts are closed to pity.

COL 192

$\mathcal{T}$he angel of God
could take them through the prison walls,
and they had no power to hold them.
We have the same God to-day,
and he works on the same plan.

RH 22 April 1890

Angels mention that sacred name with the greatest awe,
ever veiling their faces when they speak the name of God;
and the name of Christ is so sacred to them
that they speak it with the greatest reverence.

1 T 410

5—ANGELS

$\mathcal{A}$ngels "gather together His elect from the four winds,
from one end of heaven to the other."
Little children are borne by holy angels
to their mothers' arms.

GC 645

Again and again did John Wesley escape death
by a miracle of God's mercy.
When the rage of the mob was excited against him,
and there seemed no way of escape,
an angel in human form came to his side,
the mob fell back, and the servant of Christ
passed in safety from the place of danger.

GC 258

In this work the minister is attended
by the angels of heaven,
and he himself is instructed and enlightened in the truth
that maketh wise unto salvation.

AA 527

---

*H*eavenly beings still visit the earth
as in the days when they walked and talked
with Abraham and with Moses.

COL 176

---

*L*et us keep the heart full of God's precious promises,
that we may speak words
that will be a comfort and strength to others.
Thus we may learn the language of the heavenly angels,
who, if we are faithful,
will be our companions through the eternal ages.

SD 328

Rays from the Sun of Righteousness
bring gladness to the sick and suffering.
Angels of God are there,
and the simple faith shown
makes the crust of bread and the cup of water
as a banquet of luxury.

WM 169

Only the sense of God's presence can banish the fear that,
for the timid child, would make life a burden.
Let him fix in his memory the promise,
"The angel of the Lord encampeth round about them
that fear Him, and delivereth them." Psalm 34:7.

Ed 255

$\mathscr{E}$very child of God
should be actively engaged in helping others.
As those who have an understanding of Bible truth
try to seek out the men and women
who are longing for light,
angels of God will attend them.
And where angels go, none need fear to move forward.

PK 171

*H*oly angels are on the track
of every one of us.

RH 30 June 1896

Again and again have angels talked with men,
as man speaketh with a friend,
and led them to places of security.

LS 290

Adam, Noah, Abraham, Isaac, Jacob, and Moses
understood the gospel.
They looked for salvation
through man's Substitute and Surety.
These holy men of old held communion with the Saviour
who was to come to our world in human flesh;
and some of them talked with Christ
and heavenly angels face to face.

PP 366

Heavenly beings are appointed to do their work
of ministry—to guide, guard, and control
those who shall be heirs of salvation. . . .
Faithful sentinels are on guard
to direct souls in right paths.

ML 303

Angels are sent to minister to the children of God
who are physically blind.
Angels guard their steps
and save them from a thousand dangers,
which, unknown to them, beset their path.

3T 516

Thirty-two candidates were buried with their Lord
in baptism, and arose to walk in newness of life.
This was a scene that angels of God witnessed with joy.

Ev 315

Ten thousand times ten thousand,
and thousands of thousands of angels,
the beautiful and triumphant sons of God,
possessing surpassing loveliness and glory,
will escort Him on His way.

DA 739

I saw that the angels of God
would lead His people no faster than they could receive
and act upon the important truths
that are communicated to them.

1 T 207

The angels of heaven do not come to the earth to rule,
and to exact homage, but as messengers of mercy,
to co-operate with men in uplifting humanity.

DA 550

Angels work harmoniously.
Perfect order characterizes all their movements.
The more closely we imitate
the harmony and order of the angelic host,
the more successful will be the efforts
of these heavenly agents in our behalf.

TM 28

Though the rulers of this world know it not,
yet often in their councils angels have been spokesmen.
Human eyes have looked upon them.
Human ears have listened to their appeals.

Ed 305

In the council hall and the court of justice,
heavenly messengers have pleaded the cause
of the persecuted and oppressed.
They have defeated purposes and arrested evils
that would have brought wrong and suffering
to God's children.

Ed 305

Train the children to offer their simple words of prayer.
Tell them that God delights to have them call upon Him.
Will the Lord of heaven pass by such homes
and leave no blessing there? Nay, verily.
Ministering angels will guard the children
who are thus dedicated to God.

CT 110

$\mathcal{T}$hose who labor for the good of others
are working in union with the heavenly angels.
They have their constant companionship,
their unceasing ministry.
Angels of light and power are ever near to protect,
to comfort, to heal, to instruct, to inspire.

CM 110, 111

$\mathscr{T}$he Holy Spirit, as His representative,
and the heavenly angels, as ministering spirits,
are sent forth to aid those who against great odds
are fighting the good fight of faith.

MYP 17

Angels of God will walk on either side of them,
even in this world,
and they will stand at last among the angels
that surround the throne of God.

PK 587

*A*gain and again have the encouraging words of angels
renewed the drooping spirits of the faithful,
and carrying their minds above the things of earth,
caused them to behold by faith the white robes,
the crowns, the palm branches of victory,
which overcomers will receive
when they surround the great white throne.

ML 303

$\mathcal{L}$ift up Jesus. In him is everything noble.
Contemplate God in Christ.
He is surrounded with angels,
cherubim and seraphim continually behold him.
Angelic voices day and night cry before him:
"Holy, holy, holy, Lord God Almighty, which was, and is,
and is to come. . . . Thou art worthy, O Lord,
to receive glory and honor and power;
for thou hast created all things,
and for thy pleasure they are and were created."

ST 30 December 1889

As they approach the gates of the city,
the angels escorting the Majesty of heaven,
in triumphant tones address the company at the portals:
"Lift up your heads, O ye gates, and be ye lifted up,
ye everlasting doors, and the King of Glory shall come in!"
The waiting angels at the gates of the city
inquire in rapturous strains, "Who is this King of Glory?"
The escorting angels joyously reply in songs of triumph:
"The Lord, strong and mighty! The Lord, mighty in battle!
Lift up your heads, O ye gates, even lift them up,
ye everlasting doors, and the King of Glory shall come in!"

Again the waiting angels ask, "Who is this King of Glory!"
And the escorting angels respond in melodious strains,
"The Lord of hosts! he is the King of Glory!"
Then the portals of the city of God are widely opened,
and the heavenly train pass in,
amid a burst of angelic music.
All the heavenly host surround their majestic Commander,
as he takes his position upon the throne of the Father.

BEcho 1 August 1887

KEY TO ABBREVIATED TITLES

AA	*The Acts of the Apostles*
AH	*The Adventist Home*
1BC, 2BC, etc.	*The Seventh-day Adventist Bible Commentary*, vols. 1-7
BEcho	*The Bible Echo*
CM	*Colporteur Ministry*
COL	*Christ's Object Lessons*
CSW	*Counsels on Sabbath School Work*
CT	*Counsels to Parents, Teachers, and Students*
DA	*The Desire of Ages*
Ed	*Education*
Ev	*Evangelism*
EW	*Early Writings*
FE	*Fundamentals of Christian Education*
GC	*The Great Controversy*
GW	*Gospel Workers*
LS	*Life Sketches of Ellen G. White*
MB	*Thoughts From the Mount of Blessings*
MH	*The Ministry of Healing*

ML	*My Life Today*
1MR	*Manuscript Releases*, vol. 1
MYP	*Messages to Young People*
PK	*Prophets and Kings*
PP	*Patriarchs and Prophets*
RH	*The Adventist Review and Sabbath Herald*
SC	*Steps to Christ*
SD	*Sons and Daughters of God*
1SG, 2SG, etc.	*Spiritual Gifts* (4 volumes)
1SM	*Selected Messages*, book 1
1SP	*Spirit of Prophecy*, vol. 1
SR	*The Story of Redemption*
ST	*Signs of the Times*
1T, 2T, etc.	*Testimonies for the Church* (9 volumes)
TM	*Testimonies to Ministers and Gospel Workers*
WM	*Welfare Ministry*